There Is No Road

THERE IS
NO ROAD

_℘_

ANTONIO MACHADO

TRANSLATED BY
MARY G. BERG & DENNIS MALONEY

WHITE PINE PRESS • BUFFALO, NEW YORK

Publication of this book was made possible, in part, by grants
from the National Endowment for the Arts and with public
funds from the New York State Council on the Arts, a State
Agency.

First Edition

Cover drawing by Araceli Sanz

Library of Congress Control Number: 2003108958

Published by White Pine Press
P.O. Box 236, Buffalo, New York 14201
www.whitepine.org

℘

Traveler, your footprints
are the only road, nothing else.
Traveler, there is no road;
you make your own path as you walk.
As you walk, you make your own road,
and when you look back
you see the path
you will never travel again.
Traveler, there is no road;
only a ship's wake on the sea.

—Antonio Machado

PREFACE

I.

Antonio Machado is regarded as one of the greatest Spanish poets of the twentieth century. Born in Seville in 1875, he is often considered, along with Juan Ramón Jimenéz and Miguel de Unamuno, part of the generation of 1898, which ushered in a new Spanish poetics as the country entered the twentieth century. At the age of eight his family moved to Madrid, where he later studied at the Institución Libre de Enseñanza, a liberal institute that supported an integrated approach to the development of the student's total nature. The founder, Francisco Giner de los Rios, had a profound effect on several generations of Spanish writers and intellectuals.

In 1903 he published his first volume of poems, *Soledades*. Machado made his living as a high school teacher of French and in 1907 took his first post in the isolated town of Soria in Castile. He stayed there for five years, married, and watched his young wife sicken and die of tuberculosis. His last year there saw the appearance of his second book, *Campos de Castilla*. Soria and the area around Castile became Machado's spiritual center. Even after he moved to Baeza and Segovia he continued to write of Soria.

He stayed in Baeza for seven years before transferring to Segovia in 1919. Segovia was only an hour from Madrid, which allowed him to escape the boredom of the country for the intellectual life of the capital. He lived in Segovia from 1919 to 1932, during which time he published his third book, *Nuevas canciones,* and began to become more active in public life writing essays on political and moral issues.

In 1932 he moved to Madrid and assumed a teaching post there. This was the exciting time just after the fall of the monarchy and the declaration of the Second Spanish Republic and much intellectual and political freedom. Machado wrote many articles in newspapers defending the Republic and its plans.

With the advent of the Civil War in 1936, Machado continued to support the cause of the Republic, writing prose but very little poetry. As the war progressed and with things going bad for the Republic, Machado moved first to Rocafort, near Valencia, and then to

Barcelona. In early 1939, as Franco's army approached, he joined the exodus of refugees crossing over the border into France. He died there a month later, on February 27, 1939, in the town of Collioure .

2.

As the title of his first book, *Soledades,* suggests, Machado was a poet of solitude. His generation had experienced Spain's defeat in the War of 1898 and saw the last vestiges of Spain's once huge empire disappear. This new prospect of diminished expectations turned both the nation and its poets inward to discover and celebrate the traditional villages, barren landscapes, and common people of the Spanish countryside. Machado understood well this need to turn inward and reestablish Spain's connection with itself and its people after the long period of expansion and conquest.

In the spare and luminous language of Machado, we find extraordinary sensitivity to place and landscape, as well as a genuine feeling for local folklore and for song as a living tradition from which to learn. His poetry is not the poetry of closed rooms but that of the open air. Many of his poems were written as the result of long walks through towns and hillsides. He often entered the inner world by first penetrating the outer world of landscapes and objects. "It is," Machado said, "in the solitude of the countryside that a man ceases to live with mirrors." Machado perfected the art of seeing. His gift was the ability to create, from the material of the other world transformed through his heart, a poem. Many of Machado's poems are a voice speaking out loud to itself and to us an on-going inner dialogue. Machado speaks of this and gives a profile of himself in his poem "Portrait."

Portrait

My childhood is memories of a patio in Seville,
and a sunny orchard where lemons ripen;
my youth, twenty years on the soil of Castile;
my story, a few events just as well forgotten.

I was never a great seducer or Romeo
—that is apparent by my shabby dress—
but I was struck by the arrow Cupid aimed at me
and loved whenever I was welcomed.

Despite the rebel blood in my veins,
my poems bubble up from a calm spring;
and more than a man who lives by rules
I am, in the best sense of the word, good.

I adore beauty and following modern aesthetics;
I've cut old roses from Ronsard's garden,
but I hate being fashionable
and am no bird strutting the latest style.

I shun the shallow tenor's ballads,
and the chorus of crickets singing at the moon;
I stop to separate the voices from the echoes,
and I listen among the voices to only one.

Am I classical or romantic? I don't know. I want
to leave my poetry as the captain leaves his sword;
remembered for the virile hand that gripped it,
not for the hallmark of its maker.

I converse with the man who is always beside me,
—he who talks to himself hopes to talk to God
            someday—
my soliloquy is a discussion with this friend,
who taught me the secret of loving others.

In the end I owe you nothing; you owe me all
         I've written.
I work, paying with what I've earned
for the clothes on my back, the house I live in,
the bread that sustains me and the bed where I lie.

And when the day arrives for the final voyage
and the ship that never returns is set to sail,
you'll find me aboard, traveling light, with few
         possessions,
almost naked, like the children of the sea.

3.

     The poems in this volume are drawn from
two sequences of Proverbs and Folksongs that
appeared in Machado's books *Campos de
Castilla* and *Nuevas canciones.* They are short
verses reminiscent in form and manner of tra-
ditional Spanish lyrics, both spoken and sung.
Machado used these brief forms of traditional

verse as vehicles for a wide range of reflections and insights. His spiritual fathers in these poems include Pythagoras and Heraclitus. These aphorisms possess a lyrical intensity and explore the many-sided self in acknowledgment of an otherness within as well as without. Some bear a similarity to zen koans and others reveal the roots of Machado's convictions for the creation of a poetry of broad social resonance.

—Mary G. Berg & Dennis Maloney

ANTONIO MACHADO

AN INTRODUCTION

Thomas Moore

Wallace Stevens described a poem as "the cry of its occasion," and I might compare it to the reverberation of a bell. When you ring a good bell, you want to hear the overtones and not the thud or whack of the initial strike. A poem is meant to resonate, to initiate thought and feeling rather than bring them to a stop.

I enjoy Antonio Machado's poetry because his poems are so bodily, so natural, and so languidly simple, and also because they never fail to surprise you into insight. Here is a professional philosopher who knows that dry, abstract conceptualization doesn't take you nearly as far into your subject as does a perceptive glance at the obvious world around you. He looks at a country or village scene and sees a natural truth that might otherwise lay hidden. He reveals the import of the ordinary, even as he remains within his sensuous representation of it.

Machado's poems discover the "natural symbolism" in nature and especially in ordinary human situations. He doesn't manufacture meaning but points to the paradox and lyricism inherent in the situations themselves. He is like a musician banging his fingers on the wooden keys of a piano and making meaningful sound out of his violence. Something in the intellectual mechanism of interpretation and analysis is missing in Machado's way of making poetry, and this effective short-circuiting is not the way of all poets. In fact,

Machado is a master of immediacy. He never lets you get any distance on the scene of the poem, and still he grants you the vision of timeless implications.

Reading him, I sometimes wonder if I am reading something like Stevens' adages or Willliam Blake's proverbs. His indulgence in paradox and circularity reminds me of Jesus, another poet of the magical naturalism school, and, of course, Emily Dickinson, who also made theology out of a garden patch and a local ring of hills.

I meant to say that I enjoy Machado, which isn't something I could honestly say about many poets I read and appreciate. Or, maybe it's that the enjoyment in Machado is sensual, whereas it might be more intellectual in another poet. He is more like good food than a great idea. At the same time, you could design your life around his poems. You wouldn't need any more advice or more insight.

I first came across Machado in translations by an informal mentor of mine, whom I met when I was nineteen. Thomas McGreevy was a paterfamilias and marriage counselor for James Joyce, D.H. Lawrence, and W. B. Yeats, and was a bosom companion of Samuel Beckett and their partners and families. He told me countless stories of his adventures with these word jugglers and taught me how to look at Velásquez. I was living in Ireland then and would meet him in Dublin at the National Gallery to receive my real education in a smoky room in the innards of the museum. Only later did I learn that he was deeply schooled in Machado.

Here are a few lines in McGreevy's translation from "Childish Dream." They have been with me for many years, offering their simple guidance:

> All the rose trees
> give their perfumes
> all the loves
> unfold love.

To have the opportunity to introduce these poems in the beautifully musical and direct translations by Mary Berg and Dennis Maloney means a great deal to me personally. It allows me to return to my Dublin youth and to an aesthetic that is as close to my ideal as I can imagine.

People sometimes complain that my writing is too simple, too light. Just recently a professor in an audience stood up and shouted that I was anti-intellectual. I was dumbfounded. I sometimes explain, not entirely without a twinkle in my eye, that after all my father was a plumber. That is true, and doubtless the true source of my simplicity. But I like to think that Machado's spirit has something to do with it. He could offer us a way out of the dry sophistication that accompanies modernism and a way beyond the sentimentality that creeps in as a reaction. His diction is perfect and his perceptions wonderfully circular and parabolic. He is what I expect a poet to be: an infinite mind disguised in a finite body.

There Is No Road

I never chased fame,
nor longed to leave my song
behind in the memory of men.
I love the subtle worlds,
almost weightless, delicate
as soap bubbles.
I like to see them paint themselves
in colors of sunlight and float,
scarlet into the blue sky, then
suddenly quiver and break.

These chance furrows,
why call them roads?
Everyone on a journey walks
like Jesus on the sea.

He who justifies our suspicions
we call an enemy, a thief of hope.
The fool never forgives the sight of the empty
          shell
he allowed the tooth of wisdom to crack open.

Our hours are minutes
when we anticipate knowledge
and centuries when we know
what it's possible to learn.

Fruit picked out of season
is worthless...
Even a fool's praise
won't make it valuable.

Of what men call virtue,
justice and kindness,
half is envy,
and the other half is not charity.

Don't waste your time
asking what you already know...
And who can respond
to questions without answers?

Man plagued by an appetite for robbery,
by inborn malice and natural craftiness,
developed intelligence and monopolized
        the earth.
And he even proclaims the truth! Supreme
        trick of war!

Envy of virtue
made Cain a criminal.
Glory be to Cain! Today vice
is what is envied most.

Eyes opened one day
to the light, only to later
turn back, blind, to the earth,
weary of looking without seeing!

The best of the good people
know that in this life
it's all a question of proportion;
a little more, a little less...

Virtue is the joy that lightens the most sober
       heart
and smooths Cato's furrowed brow.
The good man is the one who stocks,
       like a roadside inn,
water for the thirsty, wine for the drunk.

Let us all sing together: know we don't know
        anything;
We come from an arcane sea and flow into an
        unknown one...
And between the two mysteries is the serious
        enigma,
three trunks locked with a missing key.
Light illuminates nothing, the sage has
        nothing to teach.
What does the word say? Or the water in the
        rock?

Man is by nature a paradoxical beast,
an absurd animal in need of logic.
He created a world out of nothing and when
he finished said,
"Now I know the secret: everything is nothing."

Man is only rich in hypocrisy;
he relies on his ten thousand disguises
        to deceive
and uses the double key that protects his house,
to pick the lock of his neighbor.

Ah, when I was a boy, I daydreamed
about the heroes of the Iliad!
Ajax was stronger than Diomedes,
Hector stronger than Ajax,
and Achilles the strongest of all; because
he was the strongest!... Innocent boyhood ideas!
Ah, when I was a boy, I daydreamed
about the heroes of the Iliad!

The nutcracker of empty shells,
Columbus of a hundred vanities,
lives on tricks
that he peddles as truths.

Teresa, fiery soul!
St. John of the Cross, flaming spirit!
Fathers, around here it is very cold;
our tiny flowers of Jesus are dying!

Last night I dreamt I saw God
and spoke to God;
and I dreamed that God was listening...
Then I dreamt I was dreaming.

Things of men and women,
yesterday's love affairs,
I've almost forgotten them,
if they ever existed.

Don't be surprised, dear friends,
that my forehead is furrowed.
With men I live in peace, but with my
insides I am at war.

Of ten heads, nine
charge around and one thinks;
don't be surprised if a fool
cracks his head open fighting
for an idea.

Bees extract honey
from the flower, nightingales
capture melody from love;
Dante and I—forgive me, gentlemen—
we change—forgive me, Lucía—
love into theology.

Take a coal seller, a scholar,
and a poet out in the fields.
The poet will be silent and full of wonder,
the scholar will look and think...
The coal seller will probably search
for blackberries and mushrooms.
Take them to the theater,
and only the coal seller isn't yawning.
The person who prefers what is alive
to what is artificial
is the man who thinks, sings, or dreams.
The head of the coal seller
is full of fantasies.

How are
useful things useful?
Let's return to the truth;
vanity of vanities.

Every man
wages two battles:
in dreams, he struggles with God
and awake, with the sea.

Traveler, your footprints
are the only road, nothing else.
Traveler, there is no road;
you make your own path as you walk.
As you walk, you make your own road,
and when you look back
you see the path
you will never travel again.
Traveler, there is no road;
only a ship's wake on the sea.

He who hopes, despairs,
the popular saying goes.
It's true as truth!
The truth is always what
it is, and stays the truth
even if one thinks the opposite.

Heart, yesterday sonorous,
doesn't your little
gold coin jingle?
Will your strongbox
be emptied
before time breaks it?
Let's trust that
nothing of what we know
turns out to be really true.

O, faith of the meditator!
O, faith after having thought!
Only if a heart enters the world
does the human vessel overflow and the sea
swell.

I dreamed of God as a fiery forge
that softens iron,
like a forger of swords,
like a polisher of steel,
who went along inscribing on the leaves
of light: liberty, dominion.

I love Jesus, who said to us:
Heaven and earth will pass away.
When heaven and earth pass,
my word will remain.
Jesus, what was your word?
Love? Forgiveness? Charity?
All your words were
one word: awareness.

.

Consciousness takes two forms.
One is light, the other patience.
One involves shining some light
into the depths of the sea;
the other on waiting it out,
with a pole or net, waiting for
the fish, like a fisherman.
Tell me, which is better?
The consciousness of the visionary
who watches live fish
in the watery depths, fugitives
that will never be caught,
or this cursed job
of tossing up on the sand,
dead, the fish of the sea?

Empirical faith. We neither are nor will be.
All our life is on loan.
We brought nothing; we will take nothing
    away.

You say nothing is created?
It doesn't matter; with the clay
of the earth, make a cup
so your brother can drink.

You say nothing is created?
Potter, make your pots.
Create a cup. It doesn't matter
that you can't make clay.

Yes, each and every one on earth is equal:
the coach pulled by two skinny nags
bouncing along the road toward the
stations, the coach full of banal travelers,
and among them a silent man,
austere, a hypochondriac.
People tell him things and offer him wine...
And there, when they arrive, will only one
traveler get off? Or will they all have stayed
behind along the road?

It is good to know that glasses
are to drink from;
the bad thing is that we don't know
what thirst is for.

You say that nothing gets lost?
If I break
this crystal glass, I will
never drink from it, never again.

You say that nothing gets lost,
and perhaps what you say is true;
but we lose everything
and everything will lose us.

All things pass and all things remain,
but our task is to pass through,
to pass through making roads,
roads out over the sea.

To die... To fall like a drop
of sea into the immense sea?
Or to be what I've never been:
one, without shadow or dream,
a man walking alone,
with no road and no mirror?

Last night I dreamt I heard
God shout to me: Watch out!
Later it was God who was sleeping,
and I screamed back: Wake up!

Man has four things
that are no good at sea;
anchor, rudder, oars,
and the fear of going down.

Looking at my skull
a new Hamlet will say:
here is a nice fossil
of a carnival mask.

In passing, I notice that I'm growing old,
that in the immense mirror
where I was gazing proudly at myself one day,
it was quicksilver I was putting on.
Fate's hand strips away bands of the silver
from the mirror in the depths of my house
and everything is passing through it
like light through crystal.

Light of the soul, divine light,
beacon, torch, star, sun...
A man gropes his way along
carrying a lamp upon his back.

The eye you see isn't
an eye because you see it;
it's an eye because it sees you.

To converse,
first ask a question,
then...listen.

Look in your mirror for the other one,
the one who accompanies you.

Between living and dreaming
there is something else.
Guess what it is.

That Narcissus of yours
can't see himself in the mirror any longer,
because he is the mirror itself.

A new age? Is
the same forge still blazing?
Does water still flow
in the same riverbed?

Sun in Aries. My window
is open to the cold air.
—Oh, murmur of distant water!—
Evening awakens the river.

In the old town
—sturdy towers with storks—
the gregarious sound grows silent,
and from the empty field
comes the sound of water in the rocks.

Once again my attention
is held captive by water,
but by water in the living
rock of my heart.

When you hear water, can you tell
if it's water from peak or valley,
plaza, garden, or grove?

I find what I didn't seek:
lemon-balm leaves,
with their fragrance.

Don't define your limits,
don't fret about your profile;
they're only external images.

Look for your other half
who's always next to you
and is usually what you aren't.

In my solitude
I have seen very clearly
things that are not true.

Water and thirst are good,
shadows and sun are good,
honey from flowering rosemary,
honey from bare fields.

The cricket in his cage
by his tomato
sings, sings, sings.

Slowly form nice neat letters;
doing things well
is more important than doing them.

Oh empty skull!
Think of all that
went on inside you,
another Pandolfo said.

Wake up singers!
Time for the echoes to end
and the voices to begin.

Don't search for dissonance:
because, in the end, there is none;
People dance to any tune.

Quarreler, boxer
fight it out with the wind.
It's not the fundamental *I*
that the poet is searching for
but the essential *you*.

Seek a mirror in another,
but not the one to use for shaving
or coloring your hair.

The eyes you are yearning for,
don't be mistaken,
the eyes you see yourself in
—are eyes because they see you.

Christ taught—love your fellow man
as yourself —but never forget
he is someone else.

He spoke another truth:
seek the you that isn't yours
and will never be.

Don't scorn the word;
the world is noisy and silent,
poets; only God speaks.

So much lying takes place
due to a lack of imagination;
the truth, too, is invented.

Let's not be in a rush:
for the glass to overflow,
it must be filled first.

I tell time by my heart:
a time for hope
and a time for despair.

Beyond living and dreaming
what matters most
is waking up.

I thought my hearth was cold
and stirred up some ashes...
I burned my hand.

Do you know the invisible
spinners of dreams?
There are two: verdant hope
and stern fear.
They have a wager to see
who will spin fastest and most:
Hope's golden ball of yarn
or the black ball of Fear.
When we weave, we weave
with the yarn we are given.

Pythagoras said:
Sow mallow,
but don't eat it.
Buddha and Christ said:
Greet the blow of an ax,
with your fragrance, like sandalwood.
It's good to remember
the old sayings.
Their time isn't over yet.

Pay attention:
a solitary heart
is no heart at all.

If it's good to live,
then it's better to dream.
And best of all,
mother, is waking up.

When I'm alone
my friends are with me;
when I'm with them,
they seem so distant!

Poet, your prophecy?
"Tomorrow the dumb shall speak:
the heart and the stone."

THE CONTRIBUTORS

Thomas Moore is the best-sellling author of
Care of the Soul and *Soul Mates*. A psychothera-
pist with special training in archetypal psychol-
ogy (under Jungian analyst James Hillman),
mythology, philosophy, and religion, he lived
for twelve years as a monk in a Catholic reli-
gious order and has degrees in theology, musi-
cology, and philosophy. His most recent book,
The Soul of Sex: Cultivating Life as an Act of Love,
was published in 2002.

Mary G. Berg's recent translations from
Spanish include novels: *I've Forgotten Your
Name* by Martha Rivera (Dominican
Republic); *River of Sorrows* by Libertad
Demitrópulos (Argentina); and *Ximena at the
Crossroads* by Laura Riesco (Peru), as well as

stories, women's travel accounts, literary criticism, and collections of poetry, most recently poems by Carlota Caulfield and Marjorie Agosín (Chile). Her translations of stories by contemporary Cuban women writers, *Open Your Eyes and Soar*, is forthcoming from White Pine Press. She teaches at Harvard Extension and is a Scholar at the Women's Studies Research Center at Brandeis University.

Dennis Maloney is a poet and translator. His publications include a number of translations of work by Pablo Neruda: *The Stones of Chile, Isla Negra* (with Clark Zlotchew), *Maremoto/Seaquake* (with Maria Jacketti), *Windows That Open Inward* (with photographs by Milton Rogovin) and *The House in the Sand*. His translations of work by Juan Ramón

Jiménéz and Antonio Machado have also been published, as have several volumes of work translated from Japanese, including *Between the Floating Mist: Poems of Ryokan* and *Tangled Hair: Love Poems of Yosano Akiko*, both with Hide Oshiro.

COMPANIONS FOR THE JOURNEY SERIES

This series presents inspirational work by well-known writers in a small-format book designed to be carried along on your journey through life.

VOLUME 1

Wild Ways: Zen Poems of Ikkyu
Translated by John Stevens
1-893996-65-4   128 pages $14.00

VOLUME 2

There Is No Road: Proverbs by Antonio Machado
Translated by Mary G. Berg and Dennis Maloney
1-893996-66-2   112 pages $14.00

Printed in the USA
CPSIA information can be obtained
at www.ICGtesting.com
JSHW082221140824
68134JS00015B/656

9 781893 996663